The Basics of Christianity

John-William Noble

Onwards and Upwards Publishers

Berkeley House
11 Nightingale Crescent
Leatherhead
Surrey
KT24 6PD

www.onwardsandupwards.org

ISBN: 978-1-911086-16-1
Typeface: Sabon LT
Illustrations: William Fong
Graphic design: LM Graphic Design

Author's note:
Special thanks to my father John Noble and to Pastor Fred Mok for their prayers and helpful suggestions in the writing and compilation of this book.

About the Author

John-William was brought up in Peterhead, Scotland by his parents, John and Elizabeth Noble. He was raised in an environment to know and see the love of Jesus in the hearts of fallen people restored by grace. He and his younger brother Graeme regularly attended church with their parents and John-William responded to God's call and asked Jesus into his heart at the age of twelve. He also had four loving grandparents, including his 'Grandpa', Rev. William Brown, who served as Minister of St Andrew's Church in Peterhead for many years before retiring.

John-William began studying theology at the age of fifteen in secondary school, with his father being his Higher RMPS teacher guiding him through course material on Systematic Theology. This was a good foundation for him going on to study Theology at the University of Aberdeen. At the age of twenty, he felt called to serve in full-time ministry, preaching, teaching and guiding people in God's Word.

He spent many years serving in local and international ministries whilst working as a secondary school teacher in Scotland. He preached in many different church denominations and across three continents as his understanding and application of the Word of God grew. Then in 2014, John-William married his wife, Binglin Luo, whom he had met whilst serving at Charlotte Chapel in Edinburgh. John-William and Binglin have a passionate heart to reach out to the lost with a message of salvation that has so mercifully restored their relationship with the Living God. John-William was called to serve as Pastor of the Chinese Evangelical Church in Edinburgh in 2015 and is involved in preaching and teaching and many outreach ministries across the city.

Endorsements

I wholeheartedly recommend John-William's book for new Christians and people seeking to understand the basics of the Christian faith. John-William uses helpful illustrations and discusses key arguments to encourage the reader to learn for themselves about salvation, water baptism, the Church, Bible, prayer, evangelism and other hot topics such as suffering and heaven.

Simply put, I would have benefited greatly if someone would have handed me a copy of this book as a young man seeking to grapple with the truths of the Christian faith.

It is my intention to purchase a few of these books and distribute them amongst our residents in Sunnybrae, our men's recovery centre, and Benaiah, our women and mothers with children recovery centre, who are seeking to overcome substance misuse issues in their lives.

Pastor Gordon Cruden
Director of Teen Challenge North East Scotland

This book is an excellent tool to help you lay a good foundation in a new Christian's life. John-William simply explains the basics of what it means to become a follower of Jesus Christ, while giving the person being discipled responsibility for discovering God's truth for themselves.

Pastor Mark Fleming
Director for Scottish Football at Sports Chaplaincy

The Basics of Christianity is a very attractive, lucid and evangelical introduction to the Christian faith. It is solid in its content as well as systematic in its presentation. In spite of its brevity, it is rich in nourishment and thoughtful in the treatment of Bible passages. With its apt illustrations and practical life examples, it should make a step-by-step guide into the heart of Christianity. Seekers and new believers would find it a well-informed companion; teachers and pastors would find it a very useful tool.

Maureen Yeung Marshall, PhD (Aberdeen) & Professor Emerita of Biblical Studies
Evangel Seminary
Hong Kong

This book is an excellent overview of what Christians believe and how to live as a follower of Jesus. Noble's ability to paint with broad strokes a vivid landscape of Christian doctrine is impressive. His coverage ranges in topic from baptism and church leadership to suffering and the sovereignty of God.

Fred Mok
Pastor of Chinese Church of Christ
South Valley, USA

One of the challenges of modern day Christianity is the growing epidemic of easy believe-ism and cheap grace. Some churches are notorious for making decisions and not making disciples. The church's mandate in Matthew 28:18-20 is to make disciples. Dietrich Bonhoeffer said, "Christianity without discipleship is Christianity without Christ." A church that does not disciple its members is a barrier to the work of God. The prosperity gospel has turned vice into virtue. It promotes selfishness, pride and materialism. Its proponents have replaced Christlikeness with carnality. Churches are filled with people who become Christians so that they can indulge in their self-centred lifestyles. John-William Noble's book is a breath of fresh air. The Basics of Christianity cuts to the core of what it means to be a disciple, calling us to live for the Glory of God. This book is convicting, challenging and instructive. Discipleship is a process. The Basics of Christianity paves the way for a new believer to become a reproducing Christ follower. It reveals fundamentals of Christian living. It is a gospel centred, grace filled and practical book that is a gem for new believers. I highly recommend new believers to use this book if they want to grow in maturity and experience long obedience in the same direction.

Rev. Anthony Naidoo
Author, pastor, missionary and team leader for XiXiZhiLu, China
MA in Intercultural Studies, Wheaton College, USA

John-William is a man of vision and mission for perishing souls. He came to Orissa, India twice to comfort the persecuted church by his teachings and messages.

Today, Christians desperately need to know and learn how to build their Christian faith, especially emerging leaders in church. The teaching of this book is the backbone of the Christian faith and also good for every Christian servant considering the basics of Christianity; it is a master class in communicating the gospel. It is a must-read for those who are seeking God or wishing to refresh their own faith.

Divakar Undurthi
Senior Pastor
Thondangi, India

Contents

Foreword by Rev. Dr Brian Talbot 11

Note for Study Group Leaders 12

1. Are You Saved? 13

2. Why Baptism? 25

3. Church Membership 34

4. Spiritual Growth and Service 46

Conclusion 78

Supporting Materials 79

Contact the Author 80

The Basics of Christianity

Foreword by Rev. Dr Brian Talbot

One of the weaknesses in Western Christianity has often been the making of converts, rather than the instructing and training of disciples of Jesus Christ. The response by faith to the effectual call of the Holy Spirit on our lives is only the beginning of our faith journey from the present day into eternity. Providing suitable literature to instruct and guide new Christians is an important aspect of their training in Christian living so that they may mature in the faith and become effective role models to other people, who in turn will become followers of Jesus. Every committed Christian will wish to be an active participant in some form of Christian ministry.

John-William Noble has written a clear guide to follow for participants working through these basic tenets of the Christian faith. It begins by looking at the foundational biblical teaching about how we become followers of Jesus, then looks at the first step of Christian discipleship, namely baptism. The third section of the book covers the importance of church membership, something of vital importance in an age when commitment to any organization – not just churches – has been a serious issue in recent generations. The fourth section looks at spiritual gifts and service within the church, and outside it in the wider community, including overseas mission. This study is biblical, explaining clearly what God's Word teaches on these subjects. It is also practical because our faith is about how we behave, not only concerning what we believe. I am very happy to commend this publication.

Rev. Dr Brian Talbot
Minister, Broughty Ferry Baptist Church
Dundee

Note for Study Group Leaders

Session 1 can be used for a person enquiring about Christianity and can also be studied along with Session 2 for a believer who is prayerfully considering baptism.

Session 3 can also be studied for a believer who is getting baptised and will therefore be joining a church in membership.

Session 4 can be studied straight after the first three sessions or it can be used at a later date after a person has been baptised and joined a church.

SESSION ONE

Are You Saved?

In Christian circles the question "Are you saved?" is often asked, particularly for any individual who is thinking and praying about baptism. In this session we are going to explore the basics of the Christian faith and rejoice in God's purpose for our lives. Doing so, and considering this question, will act as the best preparation for thinking about whether God has called you into His kingdom and is therefore calling you to be baptised.

There is a GOD

Arguably the biggest question in the history of humanity is the one regarding the existence of a God. In Christianity, we believe that the Bible is written by men who were inspired by ALMIGHTY GOD. You only need to read a handful of pages in the Bible to see that God is everywhere.

Let's look at the following passages to help us learn more about this God.

GENESIS 1 & PSALM 24:1-2

What do these passages teach us about God as a creator?

PROVERBS 16:9 & ROMANS 8:28

What does it mean to say that God is "sovereign over all"?

ISAIAH 48:9-11 & ROMANS 11:33-36

What does the Bible say about why we were made?

God's Glory – Our Purpose

God is our creator; He is the Sovereign Lord over all. He is everlasting, He is infinite; He is holy and blameless. This means that God is the absolute expression of perfection; He is self-defined, self-existent; there is nothing before Him and nothing without Him. This is what we can learn from the Bible and read throughout Scripture; we see also that we are created for this God, to glorify His name. To 'glorify God' is to make His infinite worth publically and universally known in our praise, in our worship, in our thanksgiving, with our lives. This is why we are made. It is because God is the root cause and purpose of our meaning and existence, and life makes sense in Him and with Him.

This is an essential reality from the Bible to understand at the beginning of these sessions. It is also a crucial starting point for considering the question "Are you saved?"

Saved from What?

We are made for God. However, living on Planet Earth for just one day makes us realise that all is not as it should be. On any given day, when we read our newspaper or go on to the Internet, we read stories of murder, theft, war, bloodshed, heartache, disease and destruction. Already at the very beginning of the Bible we can see the premise of all of that.

READ GENESIS 2-3

- God has created man "in his own image".
  (1:27-28)
- Adam and Eve live in the Garden of Eden.
  (2:15)
- God commands that they don't eat from the "tree of the knowledge of good and evil".
  (2:17)
- A serpent tempts Eve and Adam to eat the fruit from this tree.
  (3:1-5)
- Eve and Adam eat the forbidden fruit and disobey God.
  (3:6-7)
- The Lord condemns the serpent and Adam and Eve for their actions.
  (3:14-19)

READ 1 JOHN 1:5 AND JAMES 1:13

How is God described in these verses?

Why is the disobedience of Adam and Eve such a big issue?

Sin

In Romans 3:23 the Apostle Paul writes, "All have sinned and fall short of the Glory of God." The reality of the consequences of the 'fall' of Adam and Eve is catastrophic for the history of humanity. In Romans 5:14, Paul writes, "Death reigned from the time of Adam..." and this is because sin entered the world when Adam and Eve gave in to temptation and saw something of greater appeal than God and His Glory, seeking to become equal with God in their pride and rebellion.

'Sin' can be understood as 'disobeying God', and this is something that every one of us does every day. We do, say and think bad things. It means that we 'fall short' of God's Glory (Romans 3:23); that is, we *lack* God's Glory. To lack the Glory of God means that we do not display the rich and infinite worth of God in our lives and instead, our own selfish, sinful desires are at the centre of our hearts. For example, God's Glory shines on this earth, but in sin we turn our back on Him and this casts a shadow over the earth, blocking God's greatness in our lives; we seek to display the things of this world, exchanging God's Glory for images of mortal man (Romans 1:23). Our focus, our purpose, our direction becomes about the sinfulness in our hearts.

In Romans 6:23 Paul writes that "the wages of sin is death". Sin results in death which is separation from any relationship with God because we lack the Glory of God, and this leads to eternal damnation (1 Thessalonians 1:9), namely, hell. Hell is the eternal experience of eternal suffering and torment. This is a biblical reality and it must be the case. As we saw earlier, God is holy, perfect and blameless. He created man for His Glory, and yet our sin means that we fall short of that. Our sin means that we are separated from this great and awesome God. Our sin means that we must be rejected by God, condemned for our sin and condemned to go to hell.

Therefore, when we ask, "Are you saved?" we are asking, "Are you saved from sin that leads to death?" (Romans 6:23)

Helpful Analogy – Our Sin

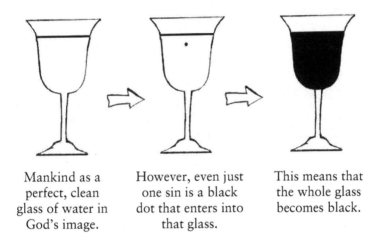

| Mankind as a perfect, clean glass of water in God's image. | However, even just one sin is a black dot that enters into that glass. | This means that the whole glass becomes black. |

We are perfect, like a clean glass of water. However, when sin enters in, it contaminates our entire being. We become sinful, blackened by sin. As a result, in our blackness, in our sin, we are no longer in God's image but man's image (Genesis 5:3). Our sin must be rejected by God. This means that despite doing some good things, living a 'generally good life', we are still sinners. We need to be saved!

There is a SAVIOUR

"Are you saved?"

"Saved from what?"

"Saved from the effects of your sin?"

Based on what we have looked at so far, we see that our purpose for being on earth is to live in relationship with our creator,

The Basics of Christianity

Almighty God, for His Glory. However, our sin has broken that relationship and we are in a desperate state. So the question is asked, "How can we be saved?"

READ JOHN 3:16-17

What has God done for us? Why?

What do you understand about Jesus?

Our Saviour Jesus

Almighty God knows that we are sinful (Ecclesiastes 7:20). Therefore, He has made a way of salvation for us. We cannot save ourselves (Romans 8:7) because our very nature is sinful and the blackness in us cannot be removed by our own efforts. This is why God sends His own Son Jesus (John 1:14) to this world to be our Saviour. Jesus comes to this earth to suffer and die on a cross (Isaiah 53) as a sacrifice for our sins.

READ ROMANS 3:25-26

- Jesus is a "sacrifice of atonement" – *at-one-ment* – Jesus, by His own choice in accordance with the will of God, brings God and mankind back together – *at one* together = *atonement.*
- Through faith "in His blood" – Jesus' blood shed on a cross is what is required.
- This demonstrates God's justice – God cannot ignore previously unpunished sins.
- Justice is attained because the penalty for our sin has been paid by our Saviour Jesus.

In Mark 10:45, Jesus says that He (the Son of Man) "did not come to be served, but to serve, and to give His life as a ransom for many". Jesus dies as a sacrifice for sins, to pay a ransom – the ransom of our sins which must be punished by a righteous and holy God.

How Can Jesus Pay for Our Sins?

Jesus is the Son of God, He is perfect (1 Peter 2:22) and He knew no sin (2 Corinthians 5:21). This is because He is God in human form, God incarnate (Colossians 1:15) and was the only one that was capable of taking away our sins. Jesus was obedient to death on a cross (Philippians 2:8) so that our sins could be nailed to Him as a perfect, living, once for all sacrifice (Hebrews 9:26). This is why Paul writes in Romans 3:25 about the blood of Jesus – because it is the blood of Jesus that is shed on the cross that is the actual "washing away of our sins" (1 John 1:7). Jesus paid the price, He paid the ransom (Mark 10:45) which is the just requirement of our sins for a holy God.

For example, imagine you are stranded on an island of sin and in the distance you see another island – a perfect island, representing heaven. In and of yourself there is no way you can get to it because of your sinful nature. However, in Jesus Christ, you have a bridge. His life, His ransom for sins becomes that bridge because all the sin of your life has been nailed to Jesus and you now have a way to get to God, through Jesus.

If...

At this point, we must stop and realise that salvation is not "salvation for all" (Matthew 7:14). In order to be saved, in order for our sins to be washed away by the blood of Jesus, we must have faith.

Faith must be understood clearly from Scripture. In Acts 16:31 we read, "Believe in the Lord Jesus and you will be saved..." Now, this has to be qualified in the context of God's Word. For example, you could meet a drunk person on the street looking for his next sexual partner who says, "I believe in Jesus." You could meet a Muslim who says, "I believe in Jesus." Even the devil believes (James 2:19). So what does it mean to *believe* in order to be *saved?*

Repent

In the Bible, there is a clear commandment to *repent* for your sins.

READ MARK 1:15, MATTHEW 3:2, ACTS 3:19

What does it mean to repent?

To *repent* does not simply mean saying sorry. To truly repent, according to God's Word, is to turn your back on your old sinful life, to make a complete U-turn, to have genuine sorrow in your heart. This can be done by realising that your life is sinful, that your wrongdoing is an offence to a righteous and holy God. Repentance means turning away from that life of sin and turning to the Lord (Acts 20:21).

Believe

Repent and *believe*. Believing in Jesus does not simply mean accepting that He has died on a cross. Believing means a genuine heartfelt belief that Jesus has died for your sins. To believe in Jesus means that you openly and joyfully accept Him and trust Him as your Saviour. In faith, we acknowledge our sinful nature and the reality that we have sinned, and we will sin, against the Lord. However, our repenting of our sins is a turning away from a heart that lives for our sinful purpose and a turning towards Jesus Christ as our Lord and Saviour.

READ 1 JOHN 5:10-13

What can this teach us about truly repenting and believing?

Confess

READ ROMANS 10:9

To confess, "Jesus is Lord!" is the open witness and declaration from the heart that you have repented of your sins and turned to Jesus, trusting in your heart that He has died for you and has saved you from your sins.

21

READ MATTHEW 10:32-33

What does Jesus call His people to do?

Our Lord Jesus commands us to, "Repent and believe the Good News!" (Mark 1:15) and to confess with our lips that "Jesus is Lord" (Romans 10:9). This confession can be described as a *witness* of one's faith, and this will take us to baptism in our later sessions.

We Are Set Free in Christ

- You are made for God's Glory.
- Sin has separated you from God.
- You are rejected by God and condemned to hell as a 'sinner'.
- God, in love, sends His Son Jesus to die for our sins.
- Jesus' blood washes away our sins if we
    1. repent of our sins;
    2. believe in Jesus as our Lord and Saviour; and
    3. confess that Jesus is Lord.

In Christ, we are *justified* by our faith (Romans 5:1) which means we are *made right* in the eyes of God. Now, we are "set free" in Christ Jesus (Galatians 5:1). This means that we are free from the damning effects of sin and free to live for God in Jesus. Almighty God no longer will look at you and turn His face away from you as a sinner because He will see the sacrifice of our Saviour Jesus which covers our sins and changes our hearts. This makes us wholly acceptable and spiritually clean before God. Therefore, God is right and just to accept us because of what Jesus has done and the faith we have in Him.

Remember the glass analogy.

Earlier we considered that our life can be pictured as a perfect glass of water that is contaminated by sin. We cannot change that because of the blackness in us. However, Jesus comes to this earth as one who is perfect and He not only covers our sins in the eyes of our Lord, but He actually changes us from within. He removes the blackness in our hearts so that we can be clean and spotless before God!

New Birth

The theological term for our salvation is a spiritual *new birth*.

READ JOHN 3:1-21

What does Jesus mean when He says that you need to be "born again" (verse 3)?

In 2 Corinthians 5:17, Paul writes that we are now a "new creation". This is because our salvation is not because of our work, but because of God's grace and Christ's work on the cross. When we *believe* by repenting of our sins and turning to Jesus, this is the response we make to the work God has graciously done in our hearts. Our faith in Jesus is the response to God's call in our lives (Ephesians 2:8) and this is a new, spiritual birth. Our old, sinful selves have died, and we are now spiritually reborn in Christ Jesus; reborn for God; reborn for His Glory!

How Do You Know You Are Saved?

We can face many doubts about whether we are actually saved.

For example:

- "Am I really a Christian or did I imagine the whole thing?"
- "If I was really changed, why do the old habits and thoughts still trouble me?[1]"
- "Why do I no longer feel the joy of my conversion so intensely? Perhaps I'm not converted after all!"
- "Why don't I have an increasing passion for God day after day?"

We must recognise that Satan prowls like a lion waiting to devour us (1 Peter 5:8) but God's Word calls us to resist the works of the enemy (James 4:7). As Christians we are emotional beings and will have 'ups and downs'. However, the truth of what we have looked at in this session remains the same. God is still God and Jesus is still your Saviour if you have repented of your sins and believe that Jesus is your Lord and Saviour.

The Spirit of Jesus at Work

In our salvation, the Spirit of Christ Jesus within us has already made big changes. The Word of God teaches us that in our salvation the Holy Spirit enters into our hearts (2 Corinthians 1:22) and is our guide and strength in life. The Holy Spirit is with us in our new birth; He creates a distaste for sinful ways (Romans 8:5) and a desire and love for people and for the ways of God and not the ways of man (Galatians 5:22-23).

So, Do You Believe This?

If so, then you are ready to journey together with the Lord as we study His call to get baptised.

---

[1] We will consider this topic in greater detail when we look at 'membership' using the foundations and theology of this first session.

SESSION TWO

Why Baptism?

READ MATTHEW 28:16-20

What does Jesus instruct His disciples to do?

We are taught to "make disciples"; that is, *followers* of Jesus. Included in this command is the instruction to *baptise* in the "name of the Father and of the Son and of the Holy Spirit".

It is vitally important to establish that baptism is commanded in the Bible, and it is commanded here by our Lord Jesus.

What is Baptism?

Baptism in its original language in the New Testament is the word *baptizo* which literally means to 'dip' or 'immerse'.

Baptism has been traditionally described as a *sacrament,* meaning that it is a ceremony of great importance within Christianity. However, to be clearer from Scripture, it is a *command* or an *ordinance* that has been given by our Saviour Jesus.

Baptism has been disputed by different church groups regarding its significance and meaning. This book contains an interpretation based on Scripture and built upon what was taught and practised in the times of Christ Jesus and following His death and resurrection.

The Mode of Baptism

As stated above, baptism means 'to immerse'. We shall see that Scripture supports this interpretation of baptism by mode of immersion for those who have put their faith in Jesus Christ.

READ MARK 1:5 & 1:9-10

- John the Baptist baptises in the River Jordan. (verse 5)
- Jesus is baptised in the River Jordan. (verse 9)
- Jesus comes "up out of the water". (verse 10)

Jesus is baptised as an adult, consenting to it, "to fulfil all righteousness" (Matthew 3:15). In so doing, He shows that He came to relate to sinful man in every way and also gives us an example of baptism to follow. This example involves Jesus being in a river of water, which would imply that He wasn't simply going to be sprinkled!

We can also see from Jesus' command in Matthew 28 that people who are to be baptised are those who have already "repented and believed".

In the Book of Acts, we have clearer examples of baptisms taking place. Every recorded baptism that gives a clear description of those being baptised refers to individuals who have "repented and believed" (Acts 2:37-41, 8:12, 36-38, 9:18, 10:47-48, 16:15, 33, 18:8, 19:5). There is no recorded evidence that a person was baptised who had not repented and believed in Jesus as their Lord and Saviour.

As we study the Scriptures to understand the meaning of baptism, it will become clearer why the mode of baptism should be the immersion of believers.

The Meaning of Baptism

READ ROMANS 6:3-4

- We are baptised into Christ Jesus.
  (verse 3)
- We are buried with Him... into death.
  (verse 4)
- Just as Christ was raised... we too may live a new life.
  (verse 4)

What does this passage teach you about the mode and meaning of baptism?

ALSO READ COLOSSIANS 2:12

Baptism by immersion is the "outward action of an inward faith". Baptism is not part of your salvation. When you are called to repent and believe in Jesus, this is the response of faith to God's saving work, Christ's saving blood on the cross. Baptism is the public declaration, the outward symbol of your salvation, of that repentance and turning to God in faith in Christ Jesus.

In the passages in Romans 6 and Colossians 2 we are taught that we are "buried" with our Saviour in baptism. Thus the person who is being baptised goes down into the water as a symbol of death; he or she has died to their own sinful self. The person being baptised does not simply stay under the water but rises from the water. This rising from the water is the symbol of our rising from the dead with Christ. We rise to a "new life" in Him. This is the new birth. Baptism symbolises this hope, this salvation. We are immersed in water because as our whole body, our whole sinful, blackened self is plunged into this water, it symbolizes how our whole being has died to sin in Christ. Our whole being then comes out of the water because it is our whole being that is raised up in the victory we have in Jesus Christ.

The beauty and the joy of baptism is the realisation that this command in Scripture symbolises your dying and rising with Christ by the washing away of your sins (Acts 22:16) which has been achieved by Christ's blood shed on the cross.

Baptism not only represents how our individual identity has changed but is also an adoption ceremony into God's family and an affirmation that we are part of the body of Christ, having a new individual and corporate identity (Galatians 3:27).

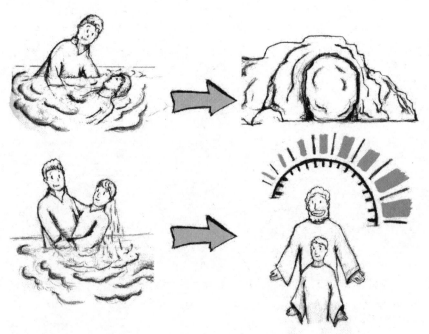

Buried with Him and raised with Him

Why do you want to be baptised?

Why do Some Churches Baptise Infants?

In some protestant churches, infants are baptised by the mode of sprinkling. The main reason for this comes from the interpretation that baptism is the symbol of the "New Covenant" (Hebrews 6:13-20). In the Old Testament, Abraham is given the promise that he will have many descendants, with male children being circumcised as a sign that the child is one of God's people under the Old Covenant (Genesis 17:10-14). In the New Testament, the New Covenant fulfilled in Christ is interpreted as being for children also.

READ COLOSSIANS 2:11-12

Why might some churches interpret that children can get baptised?

Based on the rules of the Old Covenant where circumcision marked a child as entering into the covenant community, the New Covenant symbol of baptism can be interpreted in the same way by such reasoning. In Colossians 2:11 we see a direct parallel between circumcision and baptism. Churches that baptise infants argue that the gracious love of God in the New Covenant would not exclude children and that baptism of infants is a mark that they are loved by God and that they will one day be saved. They also add that it is likely that when households of people are baptised in the New Testament (Acts 16:15,33) that there would have been children involved in these baptisms.

Criticism of this Interpretation

- In the Old Testament covenant, the circumcision of male infants was a physical means of a child entering into this covenant between God and Israel based on their being born of Jewish parents. In Scripture we can see that circumcision did not have the purpose of inward changing faith and that not all people who belonged to Israel and were Jews had an inward faith (Romans 9:6).

- The New Covenant is built upon belief in Jesus Christ as one's Lord and Saviour, which focuses on an internal change. The Old Covenant was described by Paul as a "shadow of the things that were to come" (Colossians 2:17) where physical sacrifices, temple and circumcision were the means of obedience to the law. However, the inward faith of the believer is what is "credited as righteousness" (Romans 4) and this is the change we see in the fulfilment of the law in the new covenant. Therefore, the means by which a person is baptised are not built upon the physical, but the internal. As a result, heart change is necessary and genuine saving faith evident in one's life. For this reason, the baptism of infants cannot be permitted because a child has not been "born again" (John 3).

- Baptism is described as a change of the heart, but the Bible also teaches that true circumcision is a matter of the heart (Romans 2:29). Therefore, the idea that infants were baptised in the household baptisms is purely speculative and inconsistent with scriptural teaching on the matter. Moreover, baptism performed with the assumption of future new birth / heart change / saving faith is not what is taught or takes place regarding baptism in the New Testament. Baptism is a symbol of the rebirth of a sinful being, saved by Christ and born as a new creation. The baptism of an infant cannot show this and so its purpose is very unclear.

Conclusion Regarding Infant Baptism

There are arguments from Scripture to suggest that infants could be baptised. However, these arguments are inconsistent with very clear teachings about the mode and meaning of baptism as well as not evidencing saving faith in the life of the child. Churches that baptise infants are not necessarily being heretical but it can be argued that they are theologically misinterpreting Scripture on an important matter. These churches are still our brothers and sisters but infant baptism can be argued as being a misinterpretation of Scripture.

Is Baptism Necessary?

Baptism can so easily be misunderstood. Its significance can be belittled as though it were an optional extra and yet it can also be misunderstood as having some bearing on one's salvation. As we have seen in Scripture, baptism is not an 'optional add on' to salvation, but equally it is not part of the means of salvation. Baptism as described by the Apostle Peter in 1 Peter 3:21-22 is "...not the removal of dirt from the body but the pledge of a good conscience toward God. It saves you by the resurrection of Jesus Christ, who has gone into heaven and is at God's right hand."

Is baptism necessary? You can consider Luke 23:39-43.

Am I Ready to Be Baptised?

If you have repented of your sins, confessed Jesus as Lord and Saviour and thus desire to live for God's Glory in faithful service then the answer is *yes!* Baptism is not for a stage of spiritual maturity years later. Baptism is for the believer.

This Session is not about the need to reach a deeper level of maturity in order to get baptised (although I pray that God will mature you in your walk with Him) but to ensure an understanding of salvation and so that you know the command, meaning and purpose of baptism. If this is clear in these discussions, then your 'readiness' to be baptised is very much evident.

Am I Old Enough to Be Baptised?

One final area that we must cover is the question about age. Having considered the scriptural reasons why some may baptise infants, it can be argued more strongly (and accurately) that those who were baptised and should be baptised are those that have repented and believe. So we may ask, how old must you be to be baptised?

There is no prescribed age for baptism in Scripture, just as there is no set age as to when a person can become a Christian. As soon as a person is old enough to recognise their sin and have a level of maturity to feel a genuine sorrow and desire to repent, along with an understanding, faith and love for Jesus Christ, then that person, no matter how young, can be saved.

However, this will vary, and wisdom and caution must be encouraged for parents, guardians and church leaders with children of certain ages. In the fourth session we will study discipleship and consider what it looks like to live as followers of Jesus and bear fruit for His kingdom. It is of great importance for children to show evidence and a maturity in understanding and application of what it means for them to be saved by Christ.

So, the age at which children can get baptised is not a fixed number. Rather, they need to have the following:

- An ability to understand their sin and the need to repent.
- A genuine, believable faith in Jesus Christ as their Lord and Saviour.

- Evidence of this by the way they live their lives (even at such a young age).
- Discernment from parents / teachers that know them well.

Summary

We know from Scripture that baptism is commanded by the Lord. We can also see from Scripture that it is significant for Christians to be baptised. Although it does not specifically state that people were baptised by immersion, there is very clear scriptural evidence for baptism to be baptism of believers by immersion (for example Romans 6:3-4, Colossians 2:12, Acts 22:16, Mark 1:9-10).

SESSION THREE

Church Membership

If you believe in the Almighty, Glorious God whom you were made for, have repented of your sins, confessed and believed Jesus Christ as your Lord and Saviour, and been baptised as a symbol of your inward faith in Jesus, then you can prayerfully explore the joy of joining the church!

Why Church Membership?

Why do you think it might be important to join a church?

In Scripture it is very clear that there is a marked difference between someone who is a Christian and someone who is not. As we have seen already, salvation involves heart change in Christ Jesus for a fallen sinner to repent and believe in the Good News.

However, the Bible does not specifically state that a forgiven sinner should 'join a church'. So we need to see from God's Word why it is something that is so strongly encouraged.

As Christians We Are United

Romans 12:4-5 says, "For as in one body we have many members, and the members do not all have the same function, so we, though many, are one body in Christ, and individually members one of another."

This means that every single person who becomes a Christian is joined together... in Christ.

In this world, when we support the same sport team or like the same singer or pop group, this gives us a common interest and we may come together for that purpose. Is it the same for Christians?

The Bible reveals to us that our unity is like that of a body, having various parts, meaning we are different with diverse gifts and talents. This body has a head – Jesus Christ – who gives direction and brings us together in this unique way by His blood that has been shed. This means that there is an infinitely greater significance in the togetherness of Christians to that of groups of people who share common interests.

As Christians, our togetherness is built upon eternity and our focus and meaning and purpose in life is now the same: the Glory of God.

We all move in the same direction; not simply for a few hours when we watch the same team we support, but our entire life direction and purpose is now the same. Yes, we may be different, but this is why we are described as different body parts joined together in the same body, the Body of Christ (1 Corinthians 12:27).

Individual Churches?

We can agree that to become a Christian means *change,* and that every Christian now shares something special in the salvation we have in Jesus Christ. However, we may then ask, do we need individual churches?

Practically speaking, individual churches are necessary and there is evidence of this throughout Scripture.

Paul, speaking to the leaders of the church in Ephesus, states (Acts 20:28), "Pay careful attention to yourselves and to all the flock, in which the Holy Spirit has made you overseers, to care for the church of God, which he obtained with his own blood."

Points to observe:

- There are *individual churches.* Paul writes to these churches in his letters to Corinthians, Galatians, Ephesians, Philippians, Colossians, Thessalonians. There are seven churches stated in the Book of Revelation.
- There are *overseers,* leaders of different church groups, to whom Paul writes here and elsewhere in Scripture (1 Timothy 2-3, Titus 2).
- The church is *obtained by blood* which points to the unity and headship of Jesus Christ, our chief cornerstone (Ephesians 2:19-22).

Structure in an individual church is a practical necessity due to its sheer size and the variety of gifts and abilities. We can agree that as a worldwide church we are united. However, the church is made up of smaller groups of people united in love, support and togetherness under the headship of Christ. Although the Bible does not specifically talk about joining a church, unity in studying, praying and fellowshipping together in the Lord is encouraged and practised.

In this session we will explore what it means to be part of a church as a member and how this can really strengthen the relationship we have with our Lord and our service to Him as followers of Jesus Christ.

Church Membership for God's Glory

Ephesians 3:20-21 says, "To Him who is able to do far more abundantly than all that we ask or think, according to the power at work within us, to Him be Glory in the church and in Christ Jesus throughout all generations, forever and ever."

What can we understand about the church and God's Glory from this doxology? Work through the two verses.

Breaking down the verses:

- "To Him who is able..." – This is a short exaltation of praise and Glory to God!
- "...able to do far more abundantly than all that we ask or think..." – God can do more than our very big imaginations can cope with or think up. God can do more, greater things. This is certainly absolutely true within the church. God has brought billions of lives into His church, remarkably using people in their gifts in extraordinary, God-ordained ways.
- "...according to the power at work within us..." – God is that power; the power that can enable us as His people, the church.
- "...to Him be glory in the church and in Christ Jesus." – This is it! Let's explore...

To God be the Glory... in the church! If we are set free by Christ Jesus then we have a purpose and, God willing, a desire to glorify God! Here we see in Scripture that being part of, and serving in, a church can be a significant way of living for God's Glory.

Reflection

If God is at work in every brother and sister, what practical ways can the church glorify Him in fellowship together?

The Structure of the Church

A church should be structured according to the truths and guidance of Holy Scripture as given to us by the Lord (2 Timothy 3:16). The Bible gives teaching about the way that a church is to be formed and to function.

READ 1 TIMOTHY 3:1-13, TITUS 1:5-9 & PETER 5:1-4

Leadership

The Bible teaches that the church is to have leaders. Below is a reference to the basic framework of how leaders in your church may be structured.

Elders are to be:

- *Men who are husbands of one wife* (Titus 1:6). This does not mean an elder must be married, but it is a reference to an elder's marital faithfulness in such a relationship.
- *Above reproach, self-controlled, blameless* (1 Timothy 3 & Titus 1).
- *Shepherds of God's flock,* caring and serving (1 Peter 5).
- *Not a recent convert* (1 Timothy 3:6) so therefore wisdom and experience is needed.

- *Of good reputation with outsiders* (1 Timothy 3:7) in order to be effective in leadership and reaching out with the Gospel.
- *"Able to teach"* (1 Timothy 3:2).

The role of deacons is notably different to that of elders. Deacons are not given the responsibility of overseer/teacher or to shepherd the flock. A deacon must be of godly character (1 Timothy 3:8 & 12) and this again is so crucial within the leadership and functioning of a church.

READ ACTS 6:1-7.

What are the distinguishable roles of deacons based on this passage?

How would you best describe the role of 'deacon' in the church?

Are Church Leaders Important?

As you join a church and get involved, the leadership of that church is very important for you and every member. The responsibility of a church leadership will include teaching and engaging you in the truths of the Bible and how they apply to your spiritual walk and life with Christ. Church leaders are also called by God to support you in many different practical, emotional and spiritual ways so you know that there are people with wisdom and maturity in their faith who can be trusted and are there to care for you.

For example:

Janine became a Christian nine months ago and recently joined her local church. She has started to make some friends, including the pastor and his wife. She has recently lost her job and is greatly worried about the bills that are coming through the door that she cannot pay. She shares this information with the pastor and his wife one night after having been invited for a meal and fellowship. They pray for her, share some Bible verses and in the coming weeks they offer some practical advice, continue praying for her and even recommend her to a friend who works in a similar industry and is looking for new employees. Janine is blessed by the wisdom of her pastor and the care that he shows to her in this time of need.

Church leaders have a responsibility to care for and guide the members of their congregation. This is why it is such a precious gift from our Lord to be able to be part of a church, and share in fellowship and be guided by those whom God has called to be leaders.

Can you think of any other practical ways that the church leadership could be important for you as a member of the church?

Worship

Being part of a church as a member is a gift given to us by the Lord, enabling us to join in unity and fellowship with brothers and sisters in Christ to worship and praise our Lord. This is a unique way by which we can enjoy a life of salvation in fellowship. So how do we worship the Lord as a member of church?

Church Service

- *Singing.* When we sing songs in a church service this is an act of worship (Psalm 95:1, Colossians 3:16).
- *Reading Scripture.* Studying God's Word is essential both as a way of seeking God in our church meetings and also as part of our daily lives. A church must centre itself on the guidance and teaching of Scripture.
- *Preaching God's Word.* There must be explanation and exposition of God's Word (Romans 10:14-17). The Word of God can correct, shape and guide, and the leadership of the church can be used in gifts or preaching and teaching to explain and unpack God's Word and apply it to our daily lives.
- *Prayer.* This is essential, and is modelled and taught in Scripture (1 Thessalonians 5:17, Jeremiah 33:3, Philippians 4:6 & John 16:24). It is crucial that a church service includes time to pray together. Prayer includes building a relationship with the Lord, seeking His face, trusting in Him and, most of all, worshipping and praising Him.
- *Fellowship.* A church service is the opportunity for brothers and sisters to meet and unite, growing in their togetherness in order to love and support one another.

When we come together in fellowship to worship the Lord it is known as *corporate worship.* This is the opportunity to experience the delight of praising God, growing in our knowledge and experience of Him from within the heart and sharing in this with our brothers and sisters. Being part of a church, Christ's Body, is such a precious, God-ordained way by which we can grow with the Lord together.

Church Discipline

God's Word guides us on the issue of *discipline* within the church. This topic is a necessary consideration and should bring comfort and not confusion. As forgiven sinners, we live in a fallen world and can so easily be prone to sin and be tempted by evil. The glorious blessing of a church is that God uses us as brothers and sisters to support, encourage *and rebuke* each other. This is not a means of insulting or 'knocking someone down', but a way to help every believer to move along a path of holiness in their growth with the Lord. Discipline is about guidance, support and direction towards the Lord through the Scriptures, and not about 'punishment'.

READ MATTHEW 18:15-17

What does Jesus instruct us to do?

How can this be applied to the topic of church discipline?

Church discipline is a necessary aspect of the support of a church if a brother or sister should stumble in their faith. It means that we are accountable for our actions and we put ourselves in the trust and care of the leadership of the church by becoming a member.

This is important within a church because it ensures recognition that consistent sinful behaviour and disobedience to the Word of God are not upheld or even ignored by a church community. This is a matter of holiness for the health of the church and for the brother or sister who faces such discipline.

What if a Member Ignores You?

READ 1 CORINTHIANS 5

Paul is emphasising the words of Jesus in Matthew 18 in this chapter. Here Paul stresses that if a brother refuses to listen to the guidelines of fellow church members, including the leadership of the church, then they are in effect rejecting God's guidance and should be cut off from their actual involvement within the church, namely membership.

This *does not* mean that the church should necessarily cut off any contact with this person, but circumstances must be considered and discussed for any particular situation.

For you:

By agreeing to become the member of the church, you make yourself accountable to the church as a means of entrusting the appointed people by God to guide, teach and shepherd you in your journey with Him. Church discipline can help to ensure a healthy church and the guidance and growth of your journey with the Lord.

Church Communion

Our Lord Jesus broke bread and drank wine as a symbol for His body broken and blood shed on the cross (1 Corinthians 11:23-26). This is something we are taught to do regularly in church.

Why?

It is very important to intentionally remember, reflect and meditate on what our Lord Jesus Christ has done for us, lest we forget. The knowledge of Jesus coming to this earth, reflecting the perfect Glory of Almighty God in Himself, facing the humility and humiliation of living as a man on this earth in order to die for our sins, is undoubtedly the foundation of our hope as believers in Him. To eat bread, symbolising the body of this Saviour, is a precious reminder and to do so in fellowship with other church members is crucial.

Equally, to drink wine as a symbol of Jesus' blood takes us straight to the reason for our salvation. When we drink wine, in fellowship, we take a symbol of the blood that was shed on a cross where Jesus took our sins upon Himself. The blood is the washing away of our sins and to partake in the drinking of such a symbol can bring us into corporate worship and praise to our Lord Jesus Christ.

The Benefits of Church Membership

This is a topic that we will expand in our final session.

- *Worship God.* Scripture teaches us that churches were formed and grew built upon a relationship and desire for the Living God in fellowship with each other. In 1 Corinthians 3:16 Paul asks rhetorically, "Don't you know that you yourselves are God's temple?" The church is the holy dwelling place of the Lord. It is not a building; it is a people. We are a people set apart for the Lord to display and delight in, in His absolute, glorious, infinite worth!
- *Our spiritual growth.* This is a topic we will consider in the fourth session when we study discipleship. However, it is crucial to state that church membership is a pivotal part of our growth with the Lord in faith. As stated in 1 Peter 5:2, you become part of a 'flock' and it is a truly wonderful gift given to us by the Lord to have a church leadership that can guide, support, teach and rebuke, to have brothers and sisters to share, grow with, encourage and build each other up.
- *The growth of others.* How best can we support our brothers and sisters? When we are part of a church, we will regularly meet together and have opportunities to attend services, serve together and, ultimately, grow in fellowship and together-ness. To be part of a church gives us the opportunity to be used by God in our gifts, which can naturally and so frequently benefit and support others in the church. To be

part of a church means deep, heartfelt unity. Praise God for this!

- *Outreach.*

How can the church be used to proclaim the message of Jesus Christ in the 21st century?

SESSION FOUR

Spiritual Growth and Service

As believers in Christ Jesus, saved for God's Glory, as well as being baptised and part of a church, how can we grow in our faith?

Our Daily Walk with the Lord

How do you think you can grow in your relationship with God?

Let's consider some simple but very effective steps for day-to-day living as a follower of the Lord.

Ephesians 4:15 says, "...but speaking the truth in love, we are to grow up in all aspects into Him who is the head, even Christ..."

The Bible makes it clear that as Christians we are to grow in our faith. This is *living out our salvation*. It does *not* mean we need to prove ourselves before God, but rather, that we can live in the freedom we have in Christ and the desire we have to live for Him.

God expects His children to grow in faith (1 Peter 2:2-3) and this is good and right – it enables you to enjoy your life in and for your Saviour.

In this session we will think about how we can grow in our faith and walk with Him.

Bible Reading and Study

Read the following passages and consider what they say about the importance of the Word of God.

READ 2 TIMOTHY 3:16

What does this say about the Bible?

READ EPHESIANS 6:17

Why is the Bible described in this way?

READ LUKE 8:1-15

What is the significance of God's Word in this parable?

The Bible contains God's words. It is His inspired Word. This means that it was written by man according to the *inspiration* and will of Almighty God. The Bible gives us all that we need including an understanding of who God is, the condition of our sin, the salvation revealed by faith in Christ, and the way that we can live our lives in Christ.

Tips for reading the Bible:

- *Read the Bible every day* and in a structured way. Ideally, find time in the morning to read through a section of Scripture, possibly following a daily devotional magazine, or reading through a book/section of the Bible.

- *Study the Bible.* God's Word can be difficult to understand and follow. It can be good to use helpful Bible commentaries or follow a daily devotional when studying the Bible individually. It can also be very helpful to discuss and study Scripture with brothers and sisters on a one-to-one basis or in groups. Discussing the Bible, considering what it says and learning from others, can really strengthen your handling of Scripture and your ability to interpret and understand it.

- *Meditate on the Bible.* This will be considered when we look at prayer soon. However, it is essential to know that the Bible is God's Word, and prayerfully coming to our Lord for understanding and inspiration is essential. To pray before you read Scripture, to ready your soul, can be such a blessing, as can praying and meditating on the passage after you have read it.

- *Read the Bible with expectation* because God can do mighty works in your life and through your life by His Word. Therefore, it can be helpful to ask questions about passages of Scripture that you read. For example, what does this passage teach me about God? Jesus? The Holy Spirit? My walk with the Lord? My needs? What does it tell me to do?

Prayer

READ NEHEMIAH 1

What is going on in this story?

Why does Nehemiah turn to prayer?

How does Nehemiah pray?

READ DANIEL 6:10, EPHESIANS 1:15-16, ACTS 10:9 &
2 THESSALONIANS 1:11-12

The Bible is very clear: *pray!*

In it, we see clear instructions concerning prayer, and we have countless examples of prayer and how people pray. The best example is that of our Lord Jesus.

Jesus Models Prayer

Jesus was absolutely perfect, as God incarnate, and yet He dedicated time in the midst of such business to pray to His Father.

- Jesus commanded us to pray.
  (Matthew 6:5-15)
- Jesus made time to pray.
  (Mark 6:46)
- Jesus prayed to the Father that both would be glorified.
  (John 17:1-6)
- Jesus prayed for others.
  (Luke 22:31-32, John 17:6-26)

Jesus taught His disciples how to pray and, in doing so, taught what prayer is. The closest translation of 'pray' in the English language is 'to ask'.

READ MATTHEW 7:7-11

Does this mean that we can ask for the big house, nice car, fame and success in this world? If not, then what does this passage mean?

What is Prayer?

Prayer is communication with the Lord, an opportunity to speak to God, to give Him praise, to trust Him, declare your wants and needs and those of the people around you. Prayer should be motivated by a heartfelt love for this Glorious God who created you, who loves you, who has saved you and wants to have a relationship with you. Prayer is about bringing us closer to Him and deepening our faith and strength in Him.

Prayer is:

- *Pleasing to God,* described as a "fragrant perfume rising to God" (Revelation 5:8). God delights in our prayers, when we ask for things in His name, for His purpose and ultimately for His Glory!
- *Renewing and strengthening us.* We absolutely depend upon prayer to build up our faith and guide us in life. Prayer is essential!
- *Transformational.* God wants us to pray, He listens to our prayers and He answers them (Genesis 18:23-26, James 5:17-18). This doesn't mean that God will always give us what we want, but He *will* give us what we need.

51

How to Pray

This is a difficult topic because everyone will have a different way of praying, with different times and other factors. However, there are helpful considerations that can be 'prayerfully' considered when we pray.

- *Pray regularly.* The more we pray, the more we communicate with God. That is amazing!
- *Pray using Scripture.* The Bible can guide you in what to say, especially in praying to simply worship and exalt our great God as we see in the Psalms and doxologies in the Bible (i.e. Ephesians 3:20-21 & Romans 11:33-36).
- *Pray with thanksgiving in your heart.* First, thank God for who He is and for Jesus' death on the cross saving you from your sins. Meditating on what God has done for us is precious. We can also be guided and blessed by genuinely thanking God for His innumerable blessings to us.
- *Pray with discipline and structure.* Having a weekly diary of people, countries and topics to pray for is very important. People may worry that this becomes legalistic[2], but the truth is that we are sinful and need to dedicate time to prayer lest we fall victim to a sinful path that neglects it.
- *Pray with others.* If you are married or have family, dedicate regular times to pray and study the Bible. Attending prayer meetings in church is also a vital way to listen to God and to discern His will for the life of the church and your involvement and service to Him.

READ 1 THESSALONIANS 5:16-18

Spend some time in prayer. Meditate... and rejoice!

Christian Fellowship

One other key aspect to consider in our daily walk with the Lord is Christian fellowship.

---

[2] This means following religious rules (law) as a means of gaining God's acceptance, which contradicts the teaching that we are saved completely by believing in the gracious work of Jesus Christ on the cross.

God has designed human beings to be relational beings, which means we are not made to be alone. Moreover, Christ died for our sins to bring us into relationship with God and with each other (1 John 4:7-21).

The Church as a Body

READ 1 CORINTHIANS 12:12-31

How are we to relate to each other as Christ's body? Give examples from the passage.

```
```

Jesus prayed that we should be in fellowship together (John 17:21) and we see this evidenced in such a glorious way by the early church in Acts (2:44, 4:32). We can also see in Scripture that we are commanded to meet together (Hebrews 10:24-25) whether it be in church or at home.

Fellowship with brothers and sisters, forming friendships and growing together is such a blessing from God. He has given us each other to share in the delights and the struggles of the Christian faith.

Consider:

Bob has just been hit with the tragic news that his father has cancer. He turns to his friend Joey for support. In Joey, he has a friend to pray with, one who knows him, one who can bring comfort, one who can listen, one who can weep with him.

What practical support can you give to (or receive from) a Christian friend...
...in good times?

...in bad times?

How can we get to deeper levels of Christian fellowship with each other where we can really care for and support each other's deepest needs and longings in life?

Discipleship

Discipleship means to be a follower of Jesus (Matthew 28:19-20). We are called to follow Him.

READ ROMANS 6:15-23

Why does Paul ask this question in verse 15?

Paul is teaching us in this passage that once we were "slaves to sin" but now are set free. We are set free to live for our purpose which is to *glorify God!* We do so by becoming "slaves to righteousness". This means that we are joined with our Lord and grow in a relationship with Him, in a desire for Him in obedience by following Him. *This does not earn our salvation;* Christ paid for it on Calvary. However, our faith is our obedience, and our life of salvation is the desire to follow our Lord. Praise God!

READ PHILIPPIANS 2:1-11

What is the joy of following Christ? Discuss.

How do we follow our Lord Jesus?

In Mark 8:34-38, Jesus instructs His people to "take up their cross and follow" Him. This means that we are called to be God-honouring, Christ-following, sin-defeating, death-defying, counter-cultural beings who have been saved by grace and set free for righteousness. Let's consider some practical steps to become followers of Jesus.

- *Put Jesus first in your life.* Taking up your cross does not mean that you enjoy the comfort of your salvation in the wealthy riches of the West, but in the arms of your Saviour through good and bad. Therefore, decisions are not based on worldly gain but on the furtherance of Christ's kingdom for the Glory of God!
- *Follow Jesus' example.* As we saw in Philippians 1, looking to the way Christ spoke, acted, lived is *the* way that we can live like Christ and follow Him. This is easy to say but incredibly difficult to do in a sinful world.
- *Love Jesus.* This is fairly straightforward, but get to the heart of it! If you love someone, you'll do things for that person. How much can we love and show affection for the Saviour who died for us? The Bible tells us that we are to abide in Christ and will therefore bear fruit (John 15:1-8) and we can give thanks to God that it isn't our work but our trust in Christ's work and His strength by which we can live and grow.

We can also grow in discipleship in and through our fellowship with brothers and sisters. One of the best ways to do this is to meet together to pray and study God's Word with an intentional focus of growing as disciples in Jesus. It is great to meet with brothers and sisters and form deeper relationships. However, in order to do this with a view to grow in faith, there needs to be intentionality about it.

For example:
Carol and Beth meet every week and they do pray together. However, their chat is about their love lives, their clothes, the latest gossip about the celebrities they like, and a brief chat about Sunday's sermon or the last Bible study they were at.

However...

Imagine if Carol and Beth met and began in prayer, then opened up God's Word and studied a passage together, considering what it says about God, reflecting on God's words in their lives and then shaping their discussions and their desire to be there for each other in their walks with the Lord, through prayer and fellowship. What a difference that would make!

One of many ways that we can grow in discipleship is through one-to-one fellowship in studying God's Word together. Below is a brief outline as to how two brothers or sisters (or small groups, couples) can study God's Word and grow in discipleship together.

One-to-One Ministry

One-to-one ministry can equip believers in fellowship and unity to sharpen their handling of God's Word and deepen their desire for God's Glory.

The process of one-to-one, once agreed can include:

- Praying together.
- Selecting a book of the Bible to study and how you wish to structure your studies together.
- Read the text out loud.
- Having a two-way discussion about the Bible. If this is a session with two believers, then this is not a teacher and

student scenario; it is two men or two women (or a small group) meeting to chat about the Bible and encouraging one another in their walk with the Lord.

When studying the Bible, you don't need to have done extensive reading prior to it or expect to grasp every point in the passage. However, it is good to have a rough framework to guide you. One approach is to work through a passage verse by verse and consider the following:

- The main point of the passage.
- A key verse or a point that touches your heart.
- Anything new that you have learned from the passage.
- How this passage relates to your faith and circumstances in life.

Regularly meeting to discuss the Bible and pray together, and letting this be the fuel for your conversations and fellowship, can be such a precious way to grow in your desire to follow Jesus and become a more effective disciple of the Lord Jesus Christ.

Spiritual Gifts

The Word of God teaches us that we have been given *gifts* from the Lord to serve Him.

READ 1 CORINTHIANS 12:1-11 & ROMANS 12:1-8

What gift(s) do you believe God has given to you?

How can your gifts be used for God's Glory...
...in the church?

...elsewhere (at work, at home etc.)?

Hindrances

We must be aware that our service to the Lord and our growth as followers of Jesus do not have an upward trajectory every day. There will be struggles along the way.

One of our greatest battles is that of the hindrances in our own selves, the sinful desires that we still battle against in this fallen world.

- *Dependence on self.* The Apostle Paul submitted his life to the Lord, depending upon Him. It is easy and natural to depend on ourselves, our own abilities and strength. The Bible can guide us to a deeper level of faith where we learn to depend upon God.

- *Disobedience.* We must learn to follow the ways of the Lord, even when it does not suit us or please us!
- *Love for our own glory!* Romans 1:18-32 is a passage that strikes the heart of the sinful self that exchanges God's Glory for man's glory. Let this be a warning for you as a follower of Jesus.

Evangelism

At this point we begin to think about our service to the Lord in proclaiming the Gospel and leading people to Jesus as their Lord and Saviour. As a church we can grow in fellowship and in studying God's Word, deepening our knowledge and desire for the Lord. Therefore, we have a heartfelt duty in our desire for God to proclaim the Good News of Jesus Christ.

What do you think evangelism means?

What is Evangelism?

Evangelism basically means proclaiming the Gospel (Mark 16:15) by sharing the Good News about Jesus to anyone in any location or environment. This is not the same as *mission* although evangelism is a crucial part of mission. To evangelise isn't something that only certain people are called to do. If you believe in Jesus you are called to be an evangelist (Philippians 1:6).

Why Should We Evangelise?

"He who wins souls is wise." So says Proverbs 11:30. There are literally souls on the line here! Whether we share the Gospel or not can be the difference between a person coming to know Jesus and believing in Him as their Lord and Saviour.

READ 2 PETER 3:9, ROMANS 6:23 & 2 THESSALONIANS 1:5-10

What do these passages teach us about God and the condemnation that awaits those who do not know the Lord?

READ ACTS 8:1-8

- Notice that the early church faces great trial and persecution for their faith.
  (verses 1-3)
- Their response is to preach the Gospel.
  (verse 4)
- The crowds respond.
  (verse 6)

READ 2 CORINTHIANS 5:20, ROMANS 9:1-4 & PHILIPPIANS 1:15-18

Look at the passion in Paul's words and described actions – a passion for the lost to be found!

Evangelism should be the desire in our hearts because we have found a treasure (Matthew 6:19-21) and it is worth more than anything in this world. It is the key to salvation, rescue from a sinful world and it is the only way to a relationship with the Living God...

61

through Jesus Christ. *This absolutely matters.* Are you a person who has a passionate heart to share this Good News so that the light of Christ can shine brightly in the hearts of those who don't know Him?

Let's consider practical steps by which we can evangelise.

Whom Should We Evangelise to?

Is it too general to say that we should evangelise to everyone? In truth, this is exactly what we should do (1 Peter 3:15) by being ready, willing and able to share the Good News at any given opportunity.

However, this must be qualified. We cannot go out into the street like a fisherman randomly throwing his net into the water in the hope he'll catch many fish. In reality, this will often lead to no fish caught because there was no sense of vision or direction. So... what must we do?

The first step is to pray. Pray for those general, unexpected, Holy Spirit driven moments to share the Gospel, whether at a first meeting or with a colleague you've known for ten years!

In addition, we must also seek to pray for certain people we are close to, namely family members, friends, colleagues that we know and that do not believe in Jesus as their Lord and Saviour. We must also seek to build relationships with new people as a means of sharing the Gospel with them.

Building Relationships and Genuine Love for People

The Bible makes it clear that we are to "love others" (Luke 6:31-33) and this should not simply be the God-given special love and unity we have with brothers and sisters. We can and should also have a love for those who don't know the Lord.

How can we show this love?

Don't treat non-believers as your evangelism project. Yes, you want them to be saved, but if a person feels like a project of yours and not cared for (loved) as a person then your attempts will be futile. Consider how you can practically get to know a person, building up a friendship, taking an interest in their passions and hobbies. In some cases, it may be appropriate to invite people to events, whether run by the church or not, to get to know them better, to build trust and closeness.

In what ways can you genuinely get to know someone? Discuss.

In doing so, we must be believers who are "above reproach" (1 Timothy 3:2) and ensure that we seek God's holiness in the friendships we build. This means that we can engage with people in our relationships but not get distracted or led astray by godless paths.

As you build relationships with non-believers, what are the possible dangers for your spiritual life? How can you resist this?

How to Tell People About Jesus

The big question that we have regarding evangelism is how we practically share the Good News about Jesus.

In truth, as we discern the words to say in prayer and revelation from the Lord, circumstances will differ depending on the person you are speaking to and your personality type.

1 Peter 3:15 encourages us to be ready to share the Good News of Jesus Christ. Now this must be treated with sensitivity and care. In a situation when somebody directly asks you about Christianity, whether you know them well or not, this is a blessed opportunity by God to give a clear description of the Gospel and to share the way that Jesus has worked in your life. In most other cases, it can be more difficult. Here are some ideas to consider:

- *Talk about Jesus* (when appropriate) in your conversation, referring to your time at church, Bible study etc. Jesus matters in your life and it is only natural that you would talk about this part of your life.

- When taking the opportunity to share about Jesus, *be ready to acknowledge your weakness and need for Jesus.* For example, if I share with a non-believer about my faith in Christianity then I would stress that I have so many flaws in my personality and that I daily make mistakes, which thus highlights my need for a Saviour from my sinful state. This approach can often be better received than immediately telling the other person that he or she needs to change... although this is a truth that must be revealed if they are to understand true biblical salvation.

- *Don't be too 'spiritual'.* This does not mean we are to behave as though Jesus were not our Lord and Saviour. However, if you are speaking to someone who is not acquainted with or does not believe in the Word of God, then perhaps using many quotes from Scripture or very complicated theological/religious language could prove to be quite confusing or even off-putting. Every situation is different, but we must pray for discernment about how we are to behave and act.

- *Tell them that you are praying for them.* This is a very simple way to show that you care for the person and that you believe that praying is a powerful thing to do! Saying you are praying for them can also potentially reveal the love of God through your words and actions.

- *Meet the person with another mature, older Christian.* Depending on the circumstances, this could be helpful when you need to answer difficult questions, and for support and guidance for you.

Bible Study and Follow-Up

If a person shows a willingness to explore more about the Gospel then it would be great to meet with that person continuously and propose doing a Bible study together, either as one-to-one[3] or in a small group.

Alternatively, you can look to bring the person to an organised course run by the church, especially if it is designed for Christian seekers or new believers. Discussing these situations with church leaders and mature believers would be advisable.

Not Interested

What if they are just not interested after so much effort on your part?

READ MATTHEW 10:11-15

Do you think that we should apply this text to situations where people reject the Gospel?

---

[3] For information about leading a one-to-one, see page 57.

It is difficult to know if there is ever a time when we should stop telling people about Jesus. In truth, a circumstance where we "shake the dust off" our feet would be in a situation where we have consistently spoken about the Good News but the person has shown no interest, possibly even being hostile towards you or the message. In other words, there can be times when we are no longer responsible or accountable for a person. However, it would still be worth praying for those that we no longer see or share with!

In other cases, it may be appropriate to continue to meet with the person as a friend and continue to pray for opportunities in the future. Isaiah 55:10 says that just as the earth is watered by the rain and doesn't come back empty, so it will be with God's Word going out. We can have faith in the unseen work in people's hearts, and bring souls before God and trust the work of the Holy Spirit. It is God who works even though you may plant or water a seed in someone's life (1 Corinthians 3:6).

It can be very discouraging if you invest a lot in a person and there seems to be no difference. However, the Bible calls us to persevere and have faith, for God is a God of miracles and the importance of the Good News is the difference between eternity with God and eternal damnation.

How can you battle against discouragements when sharing your faith with a person who seems to be completely disinterested?

Mission

Mission is often confused with evangelism. But what is it really?

READ MATTHEW 28:16-20

Notice in this passage that Jesus gives a calling to "make disciples of all nations". There are two points to observe:

- *A Christian is called to make disciples.* This means that mission involves evangelism but it is more than that. We are not simply to share the Gospel with unbelievers, but we are then to make disciples; that is, we have a calling to make people followers of Jesus by their salvation and on their spiritual walk with their Saviour.
- *A Christian is to make disciples of all nations.* Therefore, mission also involves crossing cultures, learning languages, taking the Gospel to the ends of the earth. Note: This does not simply mean taking the Gospel to countries, but to all people groups with their own language, culture and identity, of which there are thousands.

READ 2 CORINTHIANS 2:12-17

According to Paul, why should we 'do mission'?

Local Mission

A very popular contemporary phrase today is that every Christian is a missionary. This is in response to the call of Matthew 28 (The Great Commission) and other commands of Scripture. This is certainly not the extent of mission, but there is relevance to this. Being in mission as a Christian involves a passionate, God-centred desire to see people come to faith, to see churches planted and grow, to bring converts to maturity in faith.

How can you do mission in a local setting?

Overseas Mission

The main way that we do mission as believers is to be called by God to go to a certain place, to proclaim the Gospel and make disciples.

Paul was called out of his comfort zone to go into Gentile territories to proclaim the Gospel where it had not been heard (Acts 26:16-18, Romans 15:20). Today, brothers and sisters also feel a specific call to go to nations to reach unreached peoples with the Gospel, to spread the Good News about Jesus to the areas where the Gospel is not known or supressed.

What does a missionary do?

- He or she *prays to God about their calling in life.* As we see in Acts 26, Paul was called to go to a place through prayer and revelation by God.
- He or she *speaks to church leaders, their undershepherds* (1 Peter 5:1-4) *and those close to them* for prayer and practical support and guidance. This is a way by which such a call can be tested as God can use fellow believers to speak to hearts and discern that call.
- He or she *prays how he or she can serve.* This would involve...
    1. ...considering his or her skillset. For example, if he or she is a trained doctor then they may be called to become a medical missionary.
    2. ...thinking about a particular country or people group that he or she has a heart to serve.
    3. ...considering the ministry in mission God is calling them to do.
- He or she will then be *commissioned by the church,* a recognition of their calling to the mission field, and so that the church will pray and support them.

Are You Called to Serve in the Mission Field?

If this is an area that you feel personally called to, it is important to do further reading and chat with people who have served in mission abroad. It is an incredibly rich, blessed and cherished calling but it is full of challenge:

- Leaving your home.
- Leaving your family/friends.
- Leaving your comforts.
- Learning a new language.
- Learning a new culture.
- Being equipped in your understanding and ability to teach the Bible.
- Being equipped to face a culture/environment that doesn't know Jesus and may resent you for it.
- And much, much more!

We must support our brothers and sisters on the mission field. This topic is important; everyone has a God-given duty (and desire) to support those who are serving in overseas mission.

How can we do this?

- *Pray.* As with so much of living as a follower of Jesus, prayer is vital. Bringing before the Lord our mission partners and their work and needs is absolutely crucial.
- *Give.* Mission work can be expensive. The missionary workers require money to survive and the work often needs financial support. Therefore, we are called to give for the work of the Lord (1 Corinthians 16:1-4) which very much includes "making disciples of all nations".
- *Send.* If there are any brothers or sisters that are talking about going on mission, you can be used to encourage and help send them on their way.
- *Go.* Serving in overseas mission can involve a long-term service or it could be that God is calling you to serve on a short-term basis. Often people will go abroad to support long-term missionary workers in their ministry. This is a ministry that should be considered and prayed about in your walk with the Lord.

Suffering

A further consideration regarding our spiritual growth is when things are not going well. In Scripture we are promised and instructed to be joyful in the Lord. We might then think that the life of a Christian should be a constant upward journey of happiness and delight. However, as we know, this is a world of suffering where Christians suffer.

What do we mean by suffering?

2 Corinthians 4:8-9 says, "We are afflicted in every way, but not crushed; perplexed, but not driven to despair; persecuted, but not forsaken; struck down, but not destroyed."

Suffering is a big topic and can be understood as being any hardship or difficulty that we face in life. As a Christian, as we see from this passage in 2 Corinthians 4 and others, suffering can involve:

- Physical hardship.
- Mental struggles.
- Persecution for your faith.
- Attacks by Satan.

If this is a topic close to your heart or you have faced (or are facing) a particularly big struggle then it would be important to read further materials on this topic, whether about Christian persecution or about the suffering we face by living in a fallen world.

Here we will briefly consider *general suffering* that can cover many different forms.

Why do we suffer?

This is a *massive* question even for Christians to consider. Do we suffer because of Satan? Because of this fallen world? Because of our sin?

Why do you think we suffer?

READ ISAIAH 48:9-11 & HEBREWS 12:1-11

In these passages we can see that God has authority over suffering. This does not mean that God is the author of the bad and evil in this world, but it *does* mean that He is not separate from it.

Can you imagine living as a Christian where your suffering was because of Satan, and God was either incapable or not interested in helping or being involved?

In this passage in Hebrews 12 there is a recognition that we are to endure hardship. This means that we do face difficulties, it is not pleasant and they shouldn't make us feel happy. However, there are many comforts:

- *We are being disciplined by the Lord.*
  (verse 7)
  This doesn't mean punishment. Instead, God is using hardship to guide and direct us.

- *We are being treated as 'sons'.* This is so important. As children require discipline, so do we.
- *It is for our good, holiness.*
  (verse 10)

This passage is incredibly challenging. However, what it shows us is that we have the comfort of knowing that God is Sovereign over all, even the bad times. We may then ask, why does He allow it? But we must remember that in a fallen world, man's sinfulness and rebellion has created such conflict and unrest, and the very nature of now living for God in Christ will result in greater challenge and difficulty in a world where the cross is deemed "foolishness" (1 Corinthians 1:18). But instead of our suffering being meaningless, then, we find purpose, direction and joy in a God who guides and shapes us through trial.

For example:
A five-year-old child is not allowed to eat ice cream one night and doesn't understand why Mummy won't let him. He is annoyed and confused but he still feels loved and safe in Mummy's care.

Similarly with God, things will happen that we don't understand or can't explain. We can remember that God sees the big picture and has a genuine plan of love for our lives, wanting what is best for us; not what we want, but what we need to grow with Him and deepen in our desire for His Glory.

READ 2 CORINTHIANS 12:1-10

How does Paul react to this "thorn in his flesh"?

Is it right to ask God to remove our suffering?

God understands us and wants us to speak to Him and bring our pains and trials to Him. At times, we can rejoice when He answers our prayers by taking away our suffering. At other times, like for Paul in 2 Corinthians 12, we can rejoice all the more whilst feeling pain and tragedy because the Lord is glorified by His strength in us. This is very difficult, but as a people who are seeking God, this means that we can have a joy, a depth, an understanding that runs deeper than anything else. It doesn't take away the pain, and sometimes the pain can be severe and hit us very hard, but God is there. God, in the salvation of Jesus Christ, does not leave us alone. He is there to strengthen us, deepen our faith, comfort us in our pain and prepare us for eternal glory. Ultimately, the effects of our suffering, sin and death have been conquered at the cross. There is victory in Jesus and empathy and understanding in His love and embrace.

Remember: God sent Jesus to suffer, not even sparing His own Son. Even Jesus prayed that the hour might pass (John 12:27-28) but submitted to the Will of God and chose to suffer for the sake of your soul for the Glory of God's precious Name.

If we question why we suffer, how much more did Jesus deserve to be suffering-free? And yet He suffered more than anyone else! He faced the physical pain of life and death, the emotional tragedy of being abused, rejected and humiliated *and* He faced the horror of being separated from the Father on the cross because that was when He took our sins upon Himself. Darkness covered the earth as our sinless Saviour faced our darkness and sins. Praise God for the suffering of Jesus for us all!

Therefore, in our darkest moments, we have a Saviour who is there with us, simply as a friend, one who understands, one who can give us a hug, make us feel love when nobody else can. Jesus brings us closer to Him, deepens our dependence upon Him and gives us the faith to glorify His name because His love, His victory, His entire being is more powerful in the face of our pain and His victory becomes all the more meaningful.

Can you think of any passages in Scripture that can encourage you in the face of suffering? Think about suffering for your faith and also then think about suffering due to physical or emotional pain.

Heaven

Colossians 3:1 says, "Since, then, you have been raised with Christ, set your hearts on things above, where Christ is seated at the right hand of God."

What do you think this verse means?

Why is it important to think about heaven as a Christian?

What is Heaven?

Heaven is the "dwelling place of God" (Psalm 11:4, 1 Kings 22:19). Heaven can be understood as a spiritual home for the Lord that is outside the time and boundaries of humanity (John 18:36).

Heaven is also:

- *Eternal* (1 John 1:1-2).
- *Where Jesus went* when He rose from the dead and ascended to be with the Father (Luke 24:51).
- *Where Christ is seated* at the right hand of the Father (Ephesians 1:20-23).
- *The hope and promise* for those who have been saved by faith (John 14:1-2, 1 Corinthians 15:50-58).

Heaven is considered our *home* as Christians because this will be our eternal dwelling place with our Lord. This is a precious comfort and hope and something that can shape our actions and behaviours in this life. In John 15:19 Jesus says that we do not "belong to the world" because Christ has rescued us from this decay for the Glory of God and the eternity we can have with God.

Heaven will be *amazing!*

READ REVELATION 22

This chapter gives us an insight into the richness and delight of heaven. The language is written to help us visualise something truly incredible.

Notice that in verses 4-5 we see the pinnacle of the delight of heaven. We will *see God!* Our life is about Him and our everlasting life will be the delight of seeing Him and growing in our togetherness and union with Him forever. Isn't this amazing?

Should we look forward to heaven?

All the good things we have on earth are a foretaste of heaven, but will be infinitely greater in ways that God has planned so that our pleasure is secured by His radiating Glory without any sin or evil.

READ PHILIPPIANS 1:21-30

How does Paul feel about living in this life and being in heaven? What can this teach us?

Conclusion

The journey of a Christian is so precious and wonderful entirely because of our Lord Jesus Christ. As we have considered, to know that human beings are separated from the Living God because of sin is a frightening reality. However, not only does God love us so much that He sent His Son Jesus Christ to die for us, but He is now with us always, equipping and guiding us throughout our lives. Therefore, we can joyfully get baptised, join a church, have fellowship with other Christians and look to proclaim the Gospel, for such is the passion we have in our hearts by God's grace and mercy to us. There may be challenges, there will be suffering, but we do it all in Him who gives us strength (Philippians 4:13) for there is no greater joy than Jesus Christ our Lord.

Supporting Materials

Berkhof, Louis; *Systematic Theology;* The Banner of Truth Trust; © L.Berkhof 1939; ISBN 0-85151-056-6

Dever, Mark; *The Church: The Gospel Made Visible;* B&H Publishing Group 2012; ISBN 978-1-4336-7776-2

Grudem, Wayne; *Bible Doctrine: Essential teachings of the Christian faith;* Inter-Varsity Press 1999; ISBN 0-85111-594-2

Helm, David; *One-to-One Bible Reading;* Holy Trinity Church (Chicago) 2011; ISBN 978-1-921441-98-1

Piper, John; *Desiring God;* Multnomah Publishers, Inc.; © 1986 Desiring God Foundation; ISBN 1-59052-119-6
www.desiringgod.org

Contact the Author

To contact the author, please write to:

Chinese Evangelical Church of Edinburgh
1A Mayfield Road
Edinburgh
EH9 2NG

Or send an email to:

john-william@cece.org.uk

More information about the author can be found online:

www.ichthusedinburgh.com

Related Books by the Publisher

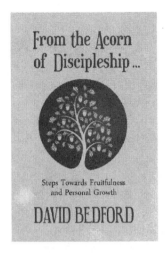

From the Acorn of Discipleship
David Bedford
ISBN 978-1-910197-28-8

This book is a passionate plea to the UK Church to return to the 'acorn' of discipleship from which will grow again the 'oak tree' of mature and powerful Jesus-centred Christianity.

In each chapter David outlines where we are as a Church, how we can improve, and practical steps we can take to grow in our faith.

It's Time to Go
Steve Mullins
ISBN 978-1-907509-88-9

In this practical, easy-to-read guide, Steve Mullins not only explains the importance of sharing Jesus with others, but also shows how we can be empowered for the task and overcome the common obstacles we face.

Books available from your local bookshop.
Or buy online at
www.onwardsandupwards.org/shop